Crate Training Puppies

Learn How to Crate Train Your Dog the Fast and Easy Way

Cesar Lopez

Published in Canada

© Copyright 2015 – Cesar Lopez

ISBN-13: 978-1511451703
ISBN-10: 151145170X

Table of Contents

Introduction

Crate training is generally recognized as one of the best ways to housetrain your puppy. Despite this, there is still a lot of reluctance among pet owners to adopt crate training as part of their training regimen, since they feel that it is in some way cruel to their pet. However, it is important to keep in mind that teaching your dog to accept temporary confinement without anxiety is an important skill for a well-behaved pet, as well as living as part of human society. If crate training is adopted humanely and responsibly, it can have many benefits for both the dog and its owner.

These include:

Providing a 'home away from home' for the pet. The crate will serve not only as a place to rest, away from a stressful environment, but also as the dog's 'den' where it can play with toys.

Establishing a regular routine that makes training easier. Since dogs will not poop where they sleep, you can take it out after it eats and it will be ready poop where you designate.

Making it easier and safer when your dog travels with you. Contrary to the impression that many movies give, the safest place for your dog is not the passenger seat of your car, but in a crate where he is in a stable environment rather than constantly bouncing around inside the vehicle. In addition, having a crate trained dog will make it easier for you to find accommodations since many hotels and motels will be willing to allow a dog if it can be crated when you are not in the room.

Ensuring the safety for a new dog. By restricting the puppy from potentially unsafe parts of the house during times when you cannot supervise it, you have an assurance that it will not chew on electric cables or get into other mischief that can be dangerous.

Restricting the dog's movements when it is not yet properly trained. For example, if you have guests over and your dog has not yet been socialized completely, you can keep your dog in the crate temporarily, or use it to introduce it to new people or pets without the risk that it will engage in aggressive or otherwise undesirable behavior such as biting and jumping.

This book will teach you everything you need to know about using crates to safely and humanely train your new puppy so that it can grow up to be a well-behaved, valued member of your family. The topics discussed in this book include:

- Choosing a crate for your puppy – what you need to keep in mind
- The right way to introduce your dog to its new crate
- What you must never do when crate training your dog

Chapter 1:
The Basics of Crate Training

Before you take your new puppy home, you should already have selected a crate so that you can start crate training immediately. The main consideration is to buy a crate that your puppy can feel comfortable in, and which allows it to stretch out and lie down as well as stand. However, the crate should not be so big that your puppy can designate a corner to poop in that is away from where he sleeps.

To help make it easier for you to choose the right crate size for your dog, here is a chart of manufacturer standards based on the weight of the dog. However, avoid taking these recommendations as absolute. You should still choose a crate based on the actual size of your dog.

Dog's Weight	Size of Crate (inch)	Examples of Breeds
Below 24 lbs	18 by 18	Chihuahua
Below 30 lbs	18 by 24	
Below 30 lbs	24 by 18	Shih Tzu, Havanese, Pekinese, Toy Poodle,
Below 38 lbs	24 by 24	Yorkshire Terrier
Below 40 lbs	24 by 30	Cocker Spaniel, Basset Hound, Dashund ,
	24 by 36	Jack Russel Terrier
Up to 40 lbs	30 by 24	Beagle, Chow Chow,
40 to 50 lbs	30 by 30	Irish Terrier, Chinese
50 to 60 lbs	30 by 36	Sharpei
40 to 60 lbs	36 by 24	Dalmatian, Old English Sheepdog,
50 to 60 lbs	36 by 30	Border Collie, American Pit Bull
60 to 80 lbs	36 by 36	Terrier
80 to 100 lbs	42 by 30	Boxer, American Bulldog, Alaskan Malamute, Airedale
	42 by 36	Tettier
80 to 90 lbs	48 by 24	Dalmatian, Boxer, Airedale Terrier, Briard, Tervueren,
80 to 100 lbs	48 by 30	Malinois
100 to 150 lbs	60 by 36	Irish Wolfhound, Newfoundland, Mastiff, Bull Mastiff, Siberian Husky, Great
150 to 180 lbs	72 by 36	Dane

If you need to measure your dog first before you buy a crate, here are the guidelines for doing so:

- To determine the maximum height of the crate, measure your puppy from the floor to its shoulder, and then add three inches for head space.
- To determine the maximum length, measure your puppy from its head to the base of its tail, and then add three inches.

If you would like to buy a crate that your dog can still use when it is fully-grown, you can get a larger crate and then use dividers to make the space inside smaller, removing them as needed. Otherwise, you will need to buy two crates, one for when your dog is a puppy and the other for when it is an adult.

Here are the different types of dog crates available:

Wire mesh crates. This is the most affordable type of crate and is essentially a cage made of hard wire. However, since it is open on all four sides, your dog may not feel that it makes a good 'den.' You can remedy this by placing a blanket on the top and three sides of the crate. To prevent the puppy from chewing on the blanket, place a plywood board on top of the crate that is around one foot longer on both sides, and then drape the blanket on top of it.

Kennel crates. This is another common type of crate, made of hard plastic, and it is covered on all sides except the front where the door is located. However, there are windows and other small openings to provide ventilation for the dog. If you plan to take your puppy on an airplane, you might want to consider this type of crate since many of them are compliant with airline requirements.

Puppy pens. This is an effective starter crate for very young dogs and has wire mesh sides, but no floor. However, this should only be used with young puppies, as older dogs may be able to move the crate and even tip it over.

Now you have to decide on the right location for the crate. Choose a place that is not too isolated but also not too busy so the dog can rest. You might also want to put it in a location where the puppy can still sense your presence, particularly at night so it does not feel anxious. Make sure that the location remains consistent and that you do not move the crate around.

Introducing Your Puppy to the Crate

Do not force the puppy to enter the crate or do anything that would make it feel anxious about the object since the puppy might not learn to consider it as a safe place. You can start by opening the door of the crate and leading the puppy to it slowly. Throw some treats inside to encourage the puppy to explore it, but otherwise do not do anything to force it to go inside the crate. Once the puppy enters the crate, lavish it with praise, but continue to stay back. At this stage, never close the door since the puppy might consequently become traumatized and ultimately fear the crate.

While the puppy is inside the crate and exploring it, speak to it soothingly and gently. Make the puppy feel safe about the crate and avoid giving the impression that he or she there to be punished. It will probably not want to stay in the crate for too long at first, so you should be sure to let it go in and out freely.

To ensure that your dog feels at home in the crate, put some dog toys and bedding inside of it, as well as other items to make it feel comfortable, such as an old shirt or other garment that has your scent on it. However, make sure that you do not put anything inside the crate that can be a choking hazard, such as toys that can be chewed into pieces and swallowed.

Once your dog has started resting inside the crate, you can begin closing the door for very short periods. However, when you initially close the door, you should make sure that you stay nearby. If your puppy starts to cry and whine, do not make a fuss about it. Just continue to talk reassuringly to it and then open the door after a few minutes. Over the course of several days or a week, gradually increase the amount of time that your dog is staying in the crate with the door closed. Do not rush it, and eventually the dog will come to see the crate as a safe place where it can go to rest and get away from stress.

Older dogs can also become used to being in a crate, but it may take a longer amount of time. What is important is that you do not force the dog to get into or stay inside the crate. Let the dog get used to being inside the crate on its own time. As with the puppy, what is important is that the dog should see the crate as something positive, and not as a cage.

From there, you can also train your dog to enter the crate on command. Decide on a cue such as 'crate', and then say it aloud, and throw a treat into the crate. Repeat this action a few times and then, once the dog associates entering the crate with a treat, say the cue word out loud, and mimic throwing a treat into the crate. Then, use your other hand to give the dog a treat once it enters he crate. Eventually, your dog will associate getting into the crate with the possibility of getting a treat, and you will not have to give it one every time.

You might also want to start feeding your dog inside the crate. If your dog has already accepted the crate, you can place the dog dish all the way into the crate. If the puppy is still anxious about the crate, you can place the dish just outside the door, or as far inside as it is willing to go. Gradually move the dish further into the crate until the puppy becomes comfortable eating completely inside of it. Once this happens, you can close the door while it is eating.

In the beginning, you should immediately open the door once the dog has finished eating and then praise the dog. Gradually increase the time the door is closed for a few minutes until it is staying in the crate for around ten minutes after eating without complaining. If the dog begins to vocalize by whining, you may be increasing the amount of time it spends in the crate too fast, and you may need to shorten this time. However, make sure you do not let the dog out when it is whining or vocalizing, since you may end up reinforcing the idea that making noise will get it out of the crate.

Your dog may start to whine or bark while in the crate. How you react to it depends on the context. If it does it at three in the morning, you should take it out to poop in the designated spot. Once the dog finishes, immediately take it back to the crate.

However, your dog may be vocalizing simply to get attention. In order to avoid reinforcing this behavior, you should ignore it. Do not scold your dog since this also represents a form of attention. Once your dog calms down, you can let it out. However, if your dog seems genuinely afraid and anxious, let it out immediately since it might injure itself by scratching the walls of the crate.

Once your dog has gotten used to being in the crate with the door closed, do not abuse the use of the crate by keeping it confined there for excessively long periods of time. At night, once the dog has learned bowel control and has a bigger bladder, you can keep it there overnight. However, during the day it should not be in there for longer than four or five hours.

If you have to keep the dog in a crate for extended periods (longer than a couple of hours), you should place a water bottle dispenser inside of it so your dog has a source of water. Here are some guidelines to follow:

- At eight to ten weeks old, the puppy should not crated longer than sixty minutes.
- At eleven to fourteen weeks old, the maximum time the puppy spends inside the crate should be between one and three hours.
- At fifteen to sixteen weeks old, the puppy should spend no more than three or four hours inside the crate.

- At seventeen weeks and older, the dog should spend a maximum of four to five hours confined in the crate.

One thing that you should never do is keep the puppy inside the crate for the whole day. Let the dog out for a break after four hours inside of the crate. If you are at work and cannot get away, ask a neighbor or hire a dog walker to let the puppy outside. In addition, you should also spend quality time with your dog in the morning before you leave for work and at night when you get home.

You might want to give your dog a thorough exercise session before putting it in the crate in the morning so that he will want to rest once he is in there.

A Word of Caution

You should only use the crate to house-train your dog or otherwise monitor destructive behavior. You should never crate your dog if it displays signs of separation anxiety since this could cause trauma and it may injure itself while in the crate. Here are some of the signs that indicate your dog may be suffering from this condition:

- Your dog exhibits destructive behavior when left alone in the house.
- Your dog soils or vocalizes thirty minutes after you leave home.
- Destroying items that have your scent, such as the sofa or doors.

Here are some other signs to look out for, indicating that your dog is suffering from an anxiety disorder and should not be crated:

- Defecation and urination inside of the crate.
- Signs inside the crate that the dog has been scratching or otherwise trying to get out.
- Excessive whining or barking when inside the crate.
- Excessive wetness on the floor or on the dog's fur that indicates it has been drooling severely.

- Attempts to move the crate while still inside.
- Damaging or attempting to damage objects that are near the crate within reach.

Furthermore, you should not confine a puppy inside a crate if:

- It does not yet have sufficiently developed bowels.
- It is vomiting or has diarrhea.
- It has not pooped before going into the crate.
- It has a high temperature.
- It has not had sufficient companionship or exercise.

Finally, avoid using the crate as a method of punishing your dog. If it is becoming a nuisance or you find it annoying, take other steps to remedy the problem and ask for professional help if you have to. While it is okay to use the crate occasionally as a way to calm the dog down temporarily, you should not make this a habit. The crate should be a pleasant place and not associated with negative experiences.

Chapter 2:
Weekend Crate Training

Trainers and dog behaviorists recommend that you should allow your dog to get used to the crate over a week, or even longer. However, if your dog is otherwise well adjusted, you can get it used to the crate more quickly. Here is a plan that you can use to teach your dog to use the crate over the course of a weekend, so that it can be confined by Monday.

Keep in mind that every dog has its own, distinct personality, and this timeline may not work for your particular pet. However, you can try this method to see if your dog will adjust quickly to being in a crate.

Preparation

Several days or weeks before starting the weekend training method, you should prepare your dog for crate training by ensuring that it is comfortable with the crate and sees it as a safe place to stay. You can do this by tossing some treats in the crate when it is not looking, so that the dog can discover them on its own and eventually become accustomed to going into the crate to look for treats.

You can also start serving the dog's meals inside the crate. If your dog is already comfortable with the crate, you can put the food dish at the back. If the dog seems reluctant to enter the crate, you can put the dish just inside the door so it will have to put its head in to eat. As your dog becomes more at ease with the crate, start moving the dish further inside until the dog becomes fully accustomed to it. Once it starts to eat, you can close the door until it finishes. Once this familiarity is established, your dog should be ready for a weekend-long training.

Sunday Morning

There is a two-stage process for training your dog to go into the crate voluntarily. The first stage, involves the dog following a treat inside the crate.

- Decide on a command or cue word that you will use when you want the dog to enter the crate.
- Use the cue word, and then throw a treat into the crate. Once the dog goes inside, give it lavish praise and give it another treat while it is still inside.
- Give your dog the cue to come out, but do not give it a treat at this stage. You want it to associate going into the crate, not running out of it, with positive experiences.

Repeat this exercise ten times, and then take a short break. Repeat another ten times before ending this stage and moving on to the next.

In the second stage, you will teach the dog to go into the crate in order to earn the treat.

- Start by doing a couple of repetitions of the previous exercise to get your dog warmed up.
- Give the command or cue word to enter the crate, but do not toss a treat inside. Point to the crate or make a motion as if throwing a treat inside so the dog will know what you want it to do.
- Once your dog follows the command, give it a treat. Finally, give the command to leave the crate.

Do this exercise ten times and then take a break. Repeat another ten times until the dog knows what it is expected to do. You will know the dog is ready for the next stage when he easily goes into and out of the crate on command.

Sunday Afternoon

During this stage, you will accustom your dog to being inside the crate while the door is closed.

- Start by getting your dog to go into the crate on command a couple of times. Give the dog a treat when it does so, and then give it the cue to exit. Do this a couple of times.

- Now you can try closing the door for a short time. When you give the command and your dog goes into the crate, praise the dog lavishly and give it a treat. Then close the door gently. Give your dog a couple of treats through the opening in the door and continue to give it praise.

- Give the cue word to exit the crate and then open the door so your dog can get out.

- If the dog seems uncomfortable or anxious, you should ease it into the situation. Instead of closing the door completely, leave it ajar and give your dog a treat. Then give the dog the cue to exit. Once the dog seems more comfortable, you can try closing the door completely.

Do this ten times. Take a short break, and then repeat this exercise another ten times, gradually increasing the time the door is closed. Vary the time the door is closed, i.e. for one repetition you can leave the dog inside for twenty seconds, in the next repetition leave it inside for five seconds, in the next fifteen and so on. Keep giving your dog treats when it is in the crate so it will feel comfortable inside. Gradually build up the time the door is closed to a minute.

Saturday Evening

Now that your dog is used to being in the crate with the door closed while you are close by, you can leave it alone for a while. Repeat the exercise described above, but latch the door so the dog cannot open it and then move away.

- Start by commanding the dog to go into the crate while you are sitting close to it. When the dog goes in, close the door and leave it closed for thirty seconds while giving the dog treats through the door. After the designated period, open the door and give it the command to exit.
- Give your dog the command to get into the crate. When the dog obeys, latch the door and give it a treat.
- Move away from the crate while giving your dog a treat. After taking a few steps away, come back and then give it a treat.
- Open the door and give the dog the command to exit.

Repeat this exercise for ten repetitions. Take a short break and then repeat for another ten times, gradually increasing the time the dog is in the crate while you move around the room. Vary the periods your dog is in the crate with every repetition, but keep returning to the crate.

Be generous with your treats at the start but slowly start tapering off with every repetition.

After repeating this exercise for two cycles of ten repetitions each, take another break. Then repeat another ten times but this time, start leaving the room for a short time. Continue to reward the dog with treats every time you come back to the crate. Work up to having the dog stay in the crate for a minute while you are walking around and then leaving the room.

Sunday Morning

During this period, you will work on getting your dog to relax in the crate for a longer period of time. Ask your dog to get into the crate and reward it with a chew bone or a toy such as a Kong that you can fill with a delicious treat like cream cheese or peanut butter. Close the door and then do an activity such as reading a book or watching TV for around half an hour. If you need to, periodically give your dog treats.

After a half hour, let the dog out of the crate but do not give it a treat. Again, the point is understanding that the crate is a positive experience. To underscore this point, you might want to ignore your dog for a while when it exits the crate. Take a break for an hour or so, and then repeat the exercise.

Sunday Afternoon

Before you start the training for the afternoon, take your dog out for some exercise. Tire your dog out so it will be more relaxed when it is in the crate.

- Command your dog to enter the crate. Once he does, close the door and give it a Kong toy or chew bone to occupy its time.
- Leave the room for ten minutes, and then come back. Give the dog the command to exit the crate and let it out. If your dog whines or vocalizes when it is in the crate, let it out only when it is quiet for a few seconds. If it has not yet finished the chew toy when it is time to exit the crate, put the toy aside.
- Take a short break and then repeat exercise.
- Keep doing the exercise throughout the afternoon, trying to work up to an hour when the dog is in the crate and you are not in the room.

Sunday Evening

Once your dog has gotten used to being alone in the crate for an hour, you can try leaving it alone in the house. Command your dog to get into the crate and then give it a chew toy or something delicious to eat that will occupy its time. Close the door and then leave the house for around ten minutes. Do not say goodbye to the dog or indicate that you are leaving.

Once you return, let your dog out of the crate and put the chew bone or treat aside. Again, remember that you should act as if there is nothing special about your dog going into and out of its crate. Repeat this exercise several times before you go to bed. Try to build up to leaving your dog alone in the house while in the crate for an hour.

At some points during the training, your dog will likely start to vocalize its complaints about being confined in the crate. What you need to do is to teach the dog that if it makes noise, you will ignore it or leave the room but if stops vocalizing, you will return and give it a treat.

- If you choose to ignore your dog, make sure that you do not give it any kind of attention that would indicate the vocalizing is having an effect. As soon as the dog falls quiet, give it a treat.
- You can also indicate to your dog by making a noise that its vocalizing will make you leave the room. Once you are gone, come back only when the dog has kept quiet for at least five to ten seconds.

If you have done the training properly, by Monday morning, you will be able to confine your dog in the crate when you leave the house. However, you should make sure that you do not confine it for longer than the recommended time. If you have to, ask a neighbor or hire a dog walker to take your dog out during lunch or after the maximum time it should spend in the crate.

Here are some other guidelines you should follow:

- Make sure you exercise your dog for thirty minutes to one hour before you put it in the crate. If you have to crate your dog for extended periods, make sure that you spend quality time with it once you let it out. Play with it and take it out for exercise when you get home or after you keep it in the crate overnight.

- Take your dog to poop before and after you ask it to go into the crate.

- Keep giving your dog its meals inside the crate. You can also reserve special treats for crate time so that your dog will be happier about going into the crate.

- If you are in the house and not crating your dog, leave the door open so it can go inside to rest if it wants to.

Chapter 3:
Housetraining Using Crates

In order to successfully housetrain your dog using crates, you will have to enlist the help of every member of the family or get a dog walker to help you while you are at work. Successful housetraining involves creating a regular routine for meals and potty breaks for your dog.

Before you start housetraining, make sure that there is no urine or residual odors inside your house since this will encourage your dog to pee in these areas. Borrow or buy a black light that will allow you to detect urine stains, and get a bottle of pet odor remover. Inspect your house using the black light and when you detect old stains, remove them using the odor remover.

Now you need to create a 24-hour routine for your dog that includes regular meal times and potty breaks in order to avoid accidents. You should also include playtime and exercise time in the schedule, as well as sleep times. Bathroom breaks should be taken every four hours, except at night when you can allow six-hour durations.

Before you prepare the schedule, however, you should observe your dog for a couple of days so that you know how long after eating it needs to go outside. Make sure you note exact times so that you can adjust the schedule.

You also need to familiarize yourself with the signs that your dog needs to go out, so that you can take it outside when it is not using the crate. The common signs include going around in a circle, looking uncomfortable or sniffing the ground. When you see these signs, you should immediately take the dog outside.

You should keep your dog on a leash when you take it outside. The impulse of the dog is not to poop right away, but to run around and explore. When the dog is on a leash, its freedom to do so is restricted so it will want to poop sooner. Be patient and when the dog finally goes, praise the dog lavishly and let it know it has pleased you. You might also want to give the dog some treats. The point here is to make your dog realize that this is where it should poop, and that doing so is a positive experience.

Once your dog poops, you can take off the leash if it is in y0ur backyard or other restricted area so it can play. Play with your dog for at least ten minutes after it poops before you take it back into the house.

Keep in mind that you should never punish your dog or treat it harshly in the event of any accidents. Doing this is cruel and can traumatize it, making housetraining more difficult. Instead, you should always use positive reinforcement to teach your dog the behavior that you want it to learn, since this will be more effective in the long run. This can also strengthen the bond between you and your dog.

Allowing Your Dog More Freedom

It is important to keep in mind that your dog should only be confined for long periods of time in a crate only during training or at necessary times such as when you are travelling and when it needs to be left alone in a hotel room. Once it is housetrained, there is no reason to keep the dog confined in the crate and you can start to give it the run of the house.

If your dog consistently poops in the designated area for at least one month and shows signs that it is housetrained and no longer demonstrates destructive behavior, you can give it more freedom. In general, depending on the personality of your dog and its particular stage of development, you can allow it more freedom at one to two years of age, or perhaps even earlier if it is well adjusted.

You can also try leaving your dog alone in the house for five to ten minutes while you step out. Make sure you dog-proof the house first before you try out this experiment. Leave out several toys for the dog to play with. If after several attempts to leave the dog alone, it continues to make a mess, this may indicate that the dog is either not yet mature enough and needs to keep being crated, or it is suffering from separation anxiety. If the latter, then you should seek professional help to remedy the problem.

Conclusion

Thank you again for choosing *Crate Training Puppies*. I hope this book was able to provide you with useful information about how to use crates humanely and responsibly to housetrain your dog. The next step is to start using the methods and techniques described in this book to start your crate training routine.

Keep in mind that training is a process that requires a lot of patience in order for it to be successful. Your dog may not respond to the training immediately and it may take some time and effort before it becomes housetrained. However, with the right training methods and a lot of tender loving care, your dog will eventually be trained and a valued member of your family.

DISCLAIMER AND/OR LEGAL NOTICES: Every effort has been made to accurately represent this book and it's potential. Results vary with every individual, and your results may or may not be different from those depicted. No promises, guarantees or warranties, whether stated or implied, have been made that you will produce any specific result from this book. Your efforts are individual and unique, and may vary from those shown. Your success depends on your efforts, background and motivation.

The material in this publication is provided for educational and informational purposes only and is not intended as medical advice. The information contained in this book should not be used to diagnose or treat any illness, metabolic disorder, disease or health problem. Always consult your physician or health care provider before beginning any nutrition or exercise program. Use of the programs, advice, and information contained in this book is at the sole choice and risk of the reader.

Made in the USA
Las Vegas, NV
30 November 2021

35658338R00024